Quite three-quarters of the plants growing in New Zealand are not to be found elsewhere: a veritable treasure store of botanical specimens that awaited European visitors who in the late eighteenth and early nineteenth centuries marvelled at the lush vegetation of our mainly evergreen forests. Unhappily the settlers who followed with fire and bulldozers to clear the land left us with only pockets of native bush with which to conjure up images of the New Zealand that was.

To the Maori, Tane, god and creator of the forest and all bird life, was the greatest and most bountiful of immortals for his wild garden provided them with their daily fare of fern-roots, birds and berries. Hence the practical needs to conserve food and other resources placed the forest under tapu, or sacredness, so that a totara tree required for a canoe could not be felled without the use of incantations, nor an expedition to snare birds be undertaken before the priest had lifted tapu restrictions.

This book summarises for the reader the salient features of some sixty most important and widely-found New Zealand trees and ferns along with brief notes on each tree's significance to the Maori people in days gone by. Peter Scaife's superb paintings draw attention to the beauty that still exists all around us and the need to ensure that what is left be preserved and fully protected.

MURDOCH RILEY

NEW ZEALAND
TREES & FERNS

NEW ZEALAND TREES & FERNS

by

MURDOCH RILEY

Illustrations by P.F. Scaife

© 1983 VIKING SEVENSEAS LTD;
P.O. Box 152, Paraparaumu
Seventh Printing 2010

NEW ZEALAND TREES AND FERNS

INDEX

AKEAKE

Dodonaea viscosa

A small tree or shrub that grows on both main islands as far south as Banks Peninsula. It prefers dry ground and reaches a height of around 7 m, with its trunk 16 cm in diameter. The tree bark is flaky and reddish-brown in colour. *Viscosa* describes the young branches that are often sticky. Akeake leaves are long, thin and willow-like with tiny petal-less flowers. Its papery seed capsules, as illustrated, are pale straw in colour with pinkish margins. The word akeake has been translated from Maori as 'forever and ever' or everlasting, referring to its hard wood, but may also denote the rustling sound made by its harsh dry leaves as they rustle against one another when set in motion by the wind.

HINAU

Elaeocarpus dentatus

One of the most handsome trees of the lowland forest,
sometimes 20 m tall and 1 m in diameter, growing in all parts
of the country. It has bright green, leathery leaves and its bark
is corrugated and loose. When its pendulous
creamy-coloured flowers appear around November
it is a beautiful sight. The 15 mm berry is purple in
colour and covered with a thin but tough skin. Before
Europeans came the Maori collected large quantities
of the berries in flax baskets and separated out the
skins and kernals by a sifting process, or steeping in
running water. The mealy matter remaining was kneaded
into cakes and baked in the umu (steam oven). The bark
made black dye.

HOHERE (Lacebark)

Hoheria populnea

Lacebark is named for the fine, net-like fibre under the bark. It is a graceful tree of medium height, reaching up some 15 m and can be 60 cm in girth. The lacebark grows on open country from North Cape to mid-North Island. It has long, broad, serrated, light green leaves, white flowers and fruit consisting of five or six seed capsules of winged nature. The inner bark of the hohere was very popular with early settlers: its tough fibre made it useful for tying up plants, in basket-work, for trimming ladies hats etc. Piupiu skirts were once made from it by the Maori, and in more recent times the same inner bark has been worn as ribbons.

HOROEKA (Lancewood)

Pseudopanax crassifolius

This small tree is found widely throughout New Zealand, from sea level up to hill country. In the mature form we illustrate, it attains a height of 12 m with a rounded head and a long, straight and naked trunk of up to 60 cm in diameter. In juvenile form, its leaves hang down, attached to the main stem like a series of fish bones attach to the spine of a fish, the so-called umbrella stage of growth, which can last for twenty years. The wood is close-grained, heavy, hard and flexible. At the adult stage the leaves are long and sharp-toothed, the flower sprays numerous, the berries small, round and black, the bark greyish. The name lancewood comes from the small 'lances' made in the wood when it is split.

HOROPITO (Peppertree)

Pseudowintera colorata

A small tree of 10 m height, or a shrub 2 m tall that can be found throughout New Zealand. The name horopito is also applied by the Maori to *Pseudowintera axillaris*, found commonly in the North Island and it is probable that the wide medicinal properties attributed to the leaves, bark and sap of the tree apply to both species. *P. colorata* has blotchy red leaves in spring time with bluish-green undersides. The buds and flowers that appear as well then are white on rich brown stems, while the ripe berries are black in colour. The hot taste of the leaves led to the name pepper tree.

KAHIKATEA (White pine)

Dacrycarpus dacrydioides

Reaching a height of 50 to 60 m, the white pine is the tallest in the country. The great length of its trunk made it, after the totara, the favourite timber of the Maori for canoes. Its timber is very light in colour and weight and was at one time used to make butter and cheese boxes. The adult tree illustrated has green scale-like leaves and fledgling yellow cones. The little orange or red oval berry fruit has its seed stuck on the top and was gathered as a food by the Maori and later by the bushman who enjoyed its sweet, if rather flavourless, taste. The berry was a favourite food too of native pigeons which the Maori easily snared on this tree.

KAIKOMAKO

Pennantia corymbosa

This small tree reaches a height of 12 m and after passing through a juvenile stage as a struggling bush with interlaced branchlets, grows a long, slender trunk of 50 cm diameter. It is found in all parts of New Zealand. The kaikomako has very fragrant white flowers of wax-like appearance that grow in profusion, the broad glossy leaves of the adult tree are 10 cm long and the berries are black-blue, the size of small plums. Because the berries were so popular with the bellbird (komako), the Maori called the tree kai (food) komako. The wood was formerly used to make a firestick which was rubbed forwards and backwards along a piece of patete or mahoe soft wood to kindle a fire by friction.

KAMAHI (Black birch)

Weinmannia racemosa

A very hardy tree found extensively from Auckland south to
Stewart Island. Kamahi grows to an average height of 25 m
with a trunk 60 to 1.2 m across. Its bark, which is grey with
white blotches, was extensively used by early settlers for
tanning leather. The Maori also used the bark to make a
red dye of permanent nature. It was regarded as an
effective preservative and fishing lines were sometimes
soaked in it to preserve them. The leaves are glossy,
dark green above and flat, light green beneath. The
small lilac-coloured flowers are very numerous on
their long stalks and the seeds that follow
are rusty-red.

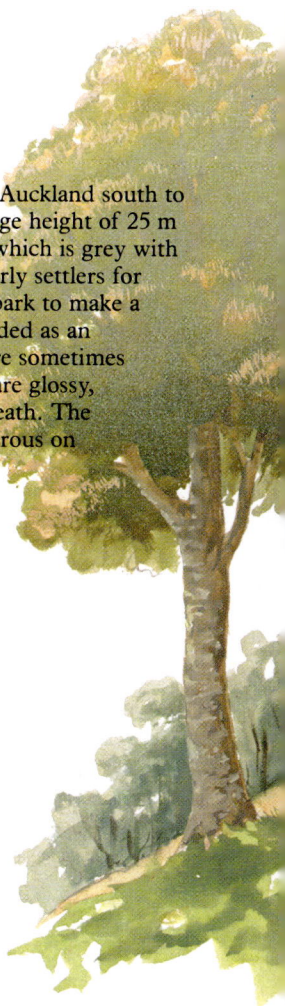

KAPUKA, PAPAUMA (Broadleaf)

Griselina littoralis

Closely related to the smaller broadleaf, Puka, this tree is distributed from North Cape to Southland and found not only at sea level but up to the sub-alpine regions, despite its name *littoralis* or shore growing. It attains a height of 17 m, is round headed with a short furrowed trunk and stout branches. The oval shaped leaves measure 1-2 cm long, are thick, green with a yellowish tinge and shiny. Kapuka has green and yellow flowers and bunches of fruit that are green until just before they are fully ripe. It can be grown from seed and cuttings take most easily. Native birds waxed fat on the berries in days of yore.

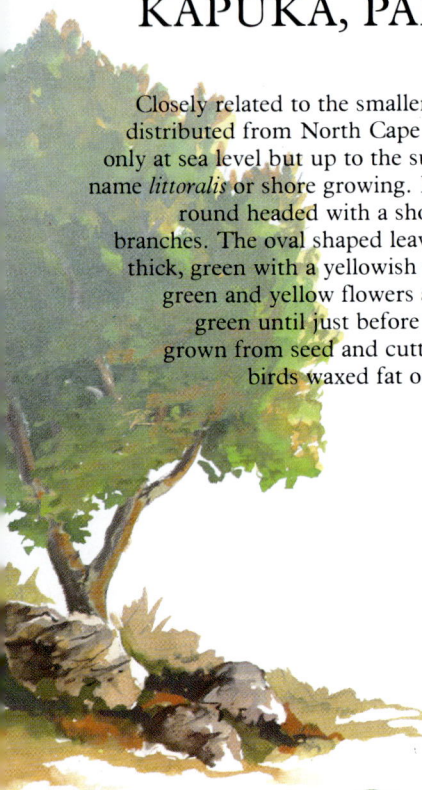

KARAKA

Cornocarpus laevigatus

Sometimes called the New Zealand laurel due to its resemblance in growth and foliage to the English laurel the karaka is claimed by the Maori to have been introduced to this country from legendary Hawaiki. In any case it is widely distributed throughout the land, reaching a height of 20 m and a diameter of 20 cm. It has large dark green and glossy leaves, the flowers are small and green. The kernels of bright orange berries, measuring 3 cm long, are very poisonous and can cause convulsions and death if eaten fresh from the tree. The Maori used a long process of steam cooking, three days and more, followed by steeping in a running stream for three months, to extract the poisonous properties.

KARAMU

Coprosma robusta

A slender trunked shrub or small tree with pale brown bark, reaching 5 m in height. It grows everywhere in forests and scrub lands, has green flowers in dense heads and sharp-pointed leathery leaves. The small orange bitter fruit drupes occur in utter profusion and have a sweet, slightly bitter taste. They were eaten by the Maori only when other fruit was unobtainable. The Maori tohunga, or priest, used branchlets of the karamu species in many religious and healing rites. These included ceremonies to ward off evil spirits, to remove spells from a person, to lift the tapu from mother and child at childbirth, and to ensure the success of the crop of kumara (sweet potato) at planting time.

KAURI

Agathis australis

New Zealand's best known tree will bear comparison with the most noble in the world. In maturity it rises majestically some 30 m with an unbranched straight trunk for perhaps two-thirds of its height. The tree is estimated to have a life-span of 2000 to 4000 years. It is found in Northland, Auckland and Bay of Plenty. Both male and female cones are found on the same branchlet, surrounded by thick, dark green leaves. The green female cone is small and round, the brown male looks like a small finger about 40 cm long. Kauri gum dug from the ground where ancient forests existed, was exported for years to make rapid drying varnishes.

KAWAKAWA

Macropiper excelsum

Found on both main islands as far south as Banks Peninsula in Canterbury, this small shrub or tree can grow up to 7 m tall. The blackish coloured branches have knotted joints, the leaves are broad, heart-shaped and jade green, the flowers have unisexual spikes, one sex only to a tree. Our illustration shows an orangish female spike and two green male spikes. The leaves, bark, root and fruit were used medicinally by the Maori for their astringent, stimulant and emollient properties. An early settler in the Nelson district related that he made a very agreeable beverage, infused like ordinary tea, from the pungent dried leaves.

KOHEKOHE

Dysoxylum spectabile

Spectabilis means beautiful, an excellent description for this forest tree of some 16 m in height that is found in the North Island and in Nelson and Marlborough. Its wood is fine-grained, of a deep red colour, and was once used in cabinet making. The long leaves look like the lily of the valley, and the fruit in their capsules with red arils, grow directly from the trunk and main branches, which is rare in New Zealand trees. The Maori sometimes cooked strong-flavoured seabirds in the leaves of the kohekohe to impart a garlic-like taste.

KOHUHU

Pittosporum tenuifolium

A small tree with black bark reaching 9 m in height,
common throughout New Zealand, excepting Westland.
The long, shiny, light green leaves attach to a darker
branchlet and are sometimes waved during the
ceremonies of receiving and welcoming visitors to a Maori
marae, the enclosed place in front of a meeting house.
The Maori also gathered a fragrant, greenish-yellow
gum the kohuhu exudes to put in the sachets that once
hung round their necks. Its flower petals are purple at
first, becoming black. At night they give off a delicate
scent. Jet black seeds are contained in a three
valve capsule.

KOROMIKO

Hebe salicifolia

There are over eighty species of *hebe* or *veronica* growing in
New Zealand, favouring high bushlands and alpine areas from
the middle of the North Island as far south as Otago. *Hebe
salicifolia* grows 4 m tall, with many branches. It has
slender pale green leaves 10 to 15 cm long which are
paired, and lilac or white flowers. Buds of the
unexpanded upper shoots were chewed by the Maori
and early settlers for diarrhoea. Like the karamu,
sprigs were used when consecrating kumara
(sweet potato) plantations to ensure a
good harvest.

KOTUKUTUKU (Tree fuschia)

Fuschia excorticata

Found growing in forest areas throughout New Zealand, the fuschia is a small tree of up to 13 m in height that is easily identified by its loose, flaky, pale reddish-brown bark and its deciduous habits — most native trees are evergreens. The flowers in North Island forms are purple and appear before the glossy leaves; in the South Island flowers can be green, turning to crimson. The berries are deep purple, juicy and sweet to eat, and were made into jam by early settlers. The Maori name of the berry is konini and when plentiful were collected by children as avidly as blackberries are today. It was the staple diet of the wild pigeon.

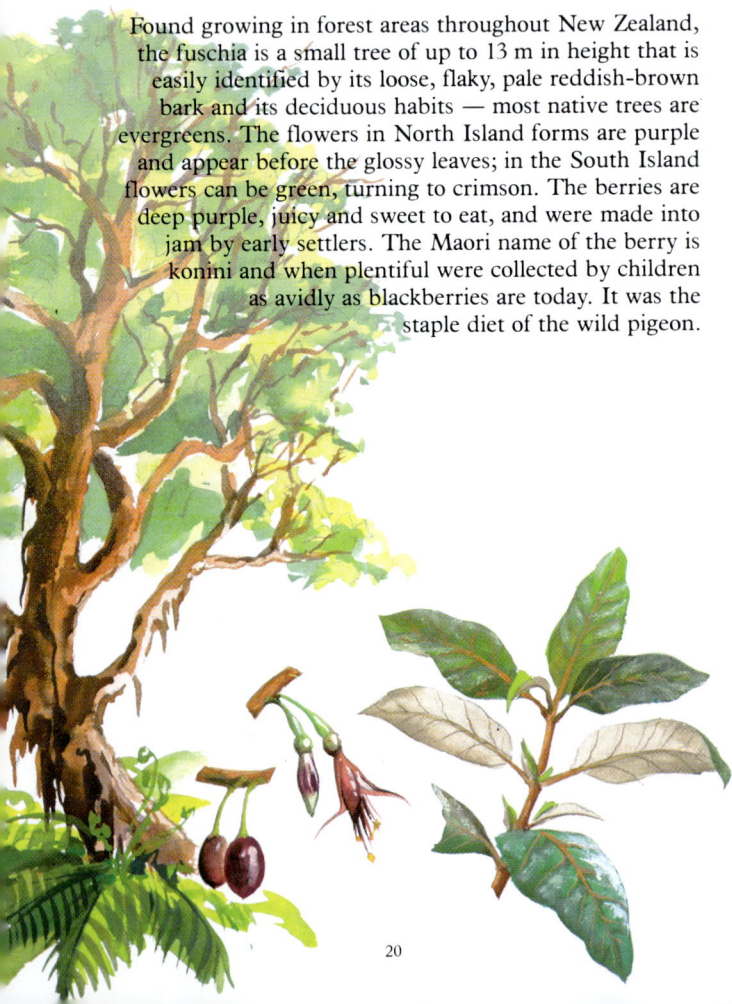

KOWHAI

Sophora microphylla

Kowhai is called New Zealand's national flower.
There are three species of kowhai that are very
similar in appearance. *Sophora microphylla*
is the most commonly seen, standing erect
with a robust trunk on open spaces, river
banks and forest edges. It grows to about
11 m tall, has tiny dull green leaves and
clusters of yellow-golden flowers borne
on chain-like branchlets. Honey from
the flowers is keenly sought by tuis and
other native birds. The long dark brown
seed pods remain on the trees for many
months. In former times the Maori made
his canoe paddles and adzes from the hard,
durable wood.

MAHOE (Whiteywood)

Melicytus ramiflorus

A round-topped small tree growing 10 m tall that is common from sea level to mountain forests throughout the land. It is a pretty sight with light green foliage, has pale bark and branches that are often encased with fungoid growth, hence the name whiteywood. The tree has tiny pale green flowers, thin serrated leaves and violet coloured berries that follow the flowers directly out of the bare branches. The flowers give off a heady fragrance, but lack nectar, hence the 'no honey' (*melicytus*) epithet given. The soft wood of the mahoe was used by the Maori in the fire-making ceremony.

MAIRE (Black maire)

Nestegis cunninghamii

Now found only in isolated forest pockets in the North Island and Nelson and Marlborough, maire was much used by the Maori as fuel in their meeting houses and huts for it gives off little smoke and has a good light. It didn't take the Europeans long to find out about its advantages as firewood too. The tree stands up to 20 m tall with a 1.5 m trunk covered in a whitish bark. It has thick but narrow leaves, very small greenish-pink flowers on short stalks, looking for all the world like open umbrellas, and crimson fruit, 1 cm long. The wood is hard, close-grained and heavy, making it ideal for Maori war clubs and canoe paddles.

MAKOMAKO (Wineberry)

Aristotelia serrata

This small graceful tree growing to 10 m high has red bark when young, becoming blacker with age. This bark is used by craftsmen to produce a black dye, as are the flowers and berries. It is to be found throughout New Zealand on the outskirts of lowland bush country and up to the sub-alpine regions. The light green leaves have deep serrations and are so thin as to appear transparent. Profuse clusters of tiny bell-like flowers adorn the tree in season, varying in colours from rose to deep red. It has currant-shaped berries that change from red to black when they are fully ripe and that are said to have a delicious flavour.

MANGEAO

Litsea calicaris

Another small tree with a compact outline, sometimes attaining 15 m in height and 50 cm in diameter. It is closely branched, has bark of a grey-brown colour and is found as far south as Rotorua in the North Island. Its special attractions are its large, sweet-scented leaves and flowers. The male and female buds open out to creamy-coloured fragrant flowers which are on separate trees in elegant sprays. Mangeao wood is light and durable, its berries reddish-purple and 2 cm long. A twig of mangeao was used by the Maori tohunga or priest in ceremonies to avert witchcraft and its tough wood made fine canoe bailers.

MANUKA (Tea tree)

Leptospernum scoparium

Manuka can be a shrub or a small tree of varying height. It grows everywhere, on rich or poor soil, and is so hardy that it is found both by the seashore and in alpine regions, often forming impenetrable thickets. The manuka is very tough and fibrous, and if broken, would never snap off, because of its sinewy consistency. The flowers are either white or rosy-tinged and like the narrow leaves have an aromatic perfume when crushed. Its light brown barks peels easily and made a kind of paint brush for the old Maori. Early settlers used the green leaves to make a fair substitute for tea, hence 'tea tree'. The seed capsules are brown and woody, opening after some years to reveal orange seeds.

MAPAU

Myrsine australis

A tall shrub or tree, attaining 7 m in height, found in open country from sea level to sub-alpine regions and quite widespread in distribution. The wood has a close, red grain and from it the Maori tohunga, or priest, had made his otaota, or staff of office. The tohunga stuck a branchlet of mapau in the ground on a kumara field as a mauri, or talisman. Its leaves are light green above, paler in colour beneath, with marked undulations and blotchy red spots. Female flowers are brown and occur in clusters on the red stems, as do the small currant-shaped berries, a favourite food of the kaka, or native parrot.

MATAI (Black pine)

Prumnopitys taxifolia

Before it became scarce, matai was an important timber
tree, reaching 30 m with its straight trunk of reddish
coloured wood. It occurs in both North and South
Islands but is rare by the coast. It is identifiable by its
thick dark grey bark that flakes off in circular chunks to
reveal scarlet patches beneath. The male and female
flowers are borne on long yellow spikes that can cover the
whole tree canopy in Spring, the tiny leaves are flat and
unpointed. Purple-black berries are produced, the size of
small plums, with a sweet taste, if of rather slimy nature.
Used by the Maori for carved feather boxes, tops,
trays and canoe prows.

MIRO

Prumnopitys ferruginea

A large forest tree of the pine family growing up to 25 m tall
and 1 m in diameter. It has a grey bark that peels off in large
flakes and red hard timber of limited value. Miro is slow in
growing and takes 400 to 600 years to reach maturity. It
prefers damp lowland forest areas and is found throughout
New Zealand. Its dark green leaves are similar to those of the
matai but have pointed rather than round tips. Male and
female flower cones are on separate trees, the fruit being
rather flattened, plum-like and with a very aromatic
turpentine flavour. The native pigeon was reputed to
wax fat on miro fruit which imparted an agreeable taste
to it at the right season.

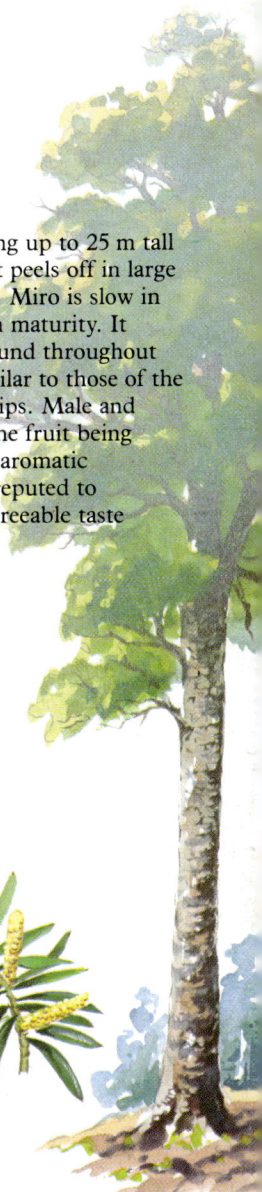

NGAIO

Myoporum laetum

Found growing near the sea in the North Island and down to Otago in the South, ngaio is a shrub or small tree reaching 10 m in height and having a fine rounded outline. Distinguishing features are its bright and glossy leaves which are light green and gland-dotted and its many heavy-looking and spreading branches of irregular form. From the leaves the Maori expressed an oil to rub on the skin to repel insect bites. It is known that cattle fed on ngaio leaves in times of scarcity have been poisoned. The flowers are white with purple spots, the nut olive-like, red to purple in colour.

NIKAU

Rhopalostylis sapida

The most tropical looking of New Zealand trees, the nikau palm is abundant at low altitudes in the North Island and south to Banks Peninsula. Its slender unbranched dark green stem may reach 12 m high and contrary to some beliefs the rings seen on its stem do not mark its age. The shiny leaves are up to 30 cm long, the pink flowers tiny and profuse on long spikes, the fruit going from green to red over the course of a year. These berries made a fine necklace for the Maori maiden and as a pellet for the European when short of ammunition and out shooting birds.

POHUTUKAWA

Metrosideros excelsa

A large, irregularly-branched tree with a short trunk that rises to 20 m tall and can be 2 m in diameter. It was established naturally only as far south as a line drawn across from north Taranaki to Poverty Bay, but has now been successfully planted as far south as Otago in the South Island. It prefers the sea coast and lake edges. The leaves are deep greenish-blue on top, white underneath. The flowers are a glorious crimson around Christmas time, hence the nickname 'New Zealand's Christmas tree'. Whitish seed capsules that follow the flowers open around May to reveal multitudes of thin brown seeds.

POROKAIWHIRI (Pigeonwood)

Hedycarya arborea

This small tree of up to 15 m high grows in the
North Island principally and in the South Island
down to Banks Peninsula and the West Coast.
Because native pigeons eat the orange fruit in
enormous quantities in season, the tree is named
pigeonwood. The tree has dark brown bark and
its hard wood was said to be the only one
suitable for the wooden drums or pahu once
struck by the Maori in cases of alarm and
audible over long distances. The leathery
leaves are glossy on top, about 10 cm long and
are coarsely toothed. The olive green flowers
are much shorter than the leaves, male and
female being on separate trees, the berries
red-gold in colour.

PUKA

Meryta sinclairii

In its natural state this small tree, reaching 9 m tall, grew only on the Three Kings and Hen and Chickens Islands when Europeans discovered it, but it has since been extensively planted in warmly situated home gardens for its attractive round head outline and broad fan-like leaves. These glossy leaves grow 30 to 50 cm long and have prominent veins and wavy margins. The flowers are greeny-yellow, male and female on separate trees in erect clusters. The fruit are purple to black when ripe. *Meryta sinclairii* belongs to the same plant family as that from which ginseng is made.

PUKATEA

Laurelia novae-zelandiae

One of the loftiest of forest trees, topping 36 m sometimes. It has little trunk to speak of, with wide buttresses on all sides that extend out from the base of the adult tree. Pukatea prefers damp forest situations and is distributed throughout the North Island and in the northern half of the South Island. The bark is pale coloured and smooth, the leaves are thick and glossy, serrated and dark green in colour. The flowers are quite small and green, tending to yellow. Around May the green fruit matures and releases silk-like seeds. The wood of the pukatea was much valued in the early days for boat building as it does not split easily.

PURIRI

Vitex lucens

A large tree of irregular growth, solid trunk and wide-spreading branches. It attains a height of 20 m and grows naturally only in the northern half of the North Island in lowland forest areas near the sea and rivers. The timber is very hard and durable, but reduced somewhat in value on account of the burrowing habits of the grub of the puriri moth. The leaves are large, varying from 5 to 13 cm long, glossy, approaching a purple-green sometimes in colour and are distinctively crinkled with smooth margins. Its pink flowers hang in groups of 4 to 15, its fruit are large and cherry red in colour. Unlike most New Zealand trees the flowers appear from mid-winter onwards.

RANGIORA

Brachyglottis repanda

The rangiora is a common small tree or shrub of some 6 m
height with sturdy brittle branches covered with a white wool
or soft hair. It grows in the North Island and northern
South Island. Abundant clusters of small fragrant flowers
that are full of honey and attract the bees stand out from
the branches. These buds and flower heads are on long
pale bracts. The very large leaves, mid-green above and
white below are poisonous to man. In days gone by
Maori raiders bound leaves of the rangiora
around their heads, white sides outwards,
so as to distinguish friend from enemy.

RATA (Northern rata)

Metrosideros robusta

The northern rata grows in the North Island and Nelson Provence to a height of 25 m, and is the big brother of the southern rata, found in Northland, but in quantity only in South Island forests. The northern rata starts out life as a climber, its wind-blown seed establishing itself high up another tree. Eventually it kills the host tree, its aerial roots disappear, though it often keeps a gnarled, contorted form in maturity. Its paired leaves are shiny at adult stage and pointed at both ends. Its flowers are red, similar in colour to those of the pohutukawa which they resemble, but smaller in size. The wood is hard and durable and takes on a deep mahogany shade of red when polished.

RAUKAWA

Pseudopanax edgerleyi

This small graceful tree reaches 10 m high and is distributed all over New Zealand in lowland forests. Raukawa has very small green flowers and equally tiny round green fruit that sometimes turn purple or black with maturity. The leaves alter in shape as the plant grows. In juvenile form three to five deeply toothed leaflets appear on one stalk; later the indentations decrease and the adult leaves, as illustrated, acquire wavy margins, and become glossy bright green above and dull green beneath. From the leaves the Maori extracted an oil to rub on their limbs and body.

REWAREWA (Honeysuckle)

Knightia excelsa

A slight, tapering, grey-barked tree, up to 30 m tall, with foliage that often starts well up the mature tree trunk and has the look of the English poplar. The adult leaves are 15 to 20 cm long, rather stiff and leathery, blunt toothed, green colour on top, brown below. Rewarewa has reddish-brown 'honeysuckle type' flowers of strong odour which attract birds like the tui who assist pollination by brushing among them. The Maori used rewarewa as firewood to char out the interior of their great totara war canoes and indeed legend has it that the rewarewa seed pod with its long boat-shape provided the inspiration for the design of the canoe.

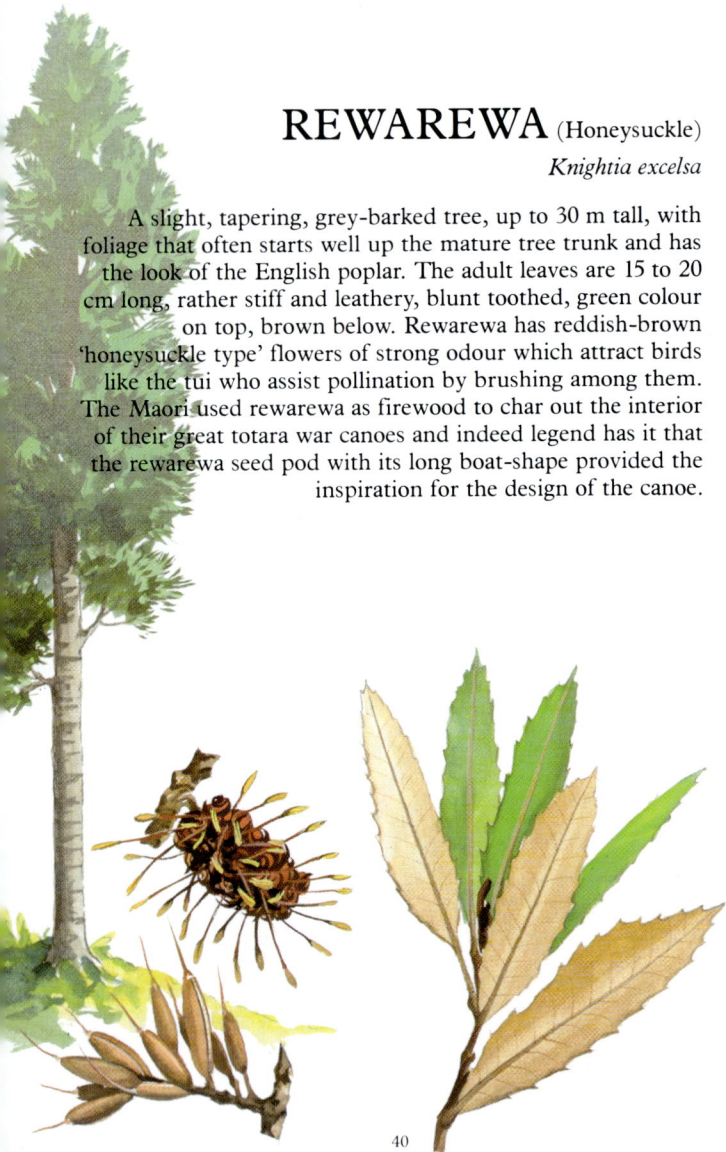

RIMU (Red pine)

Dacrydium cupressium

A pine tree heavily milled for its valuable timber but still found widely throughout New Zealand in mixed forest areas. It grows to a height of 50 to 60 m, has greyish-brown flaky bark and a trunk girth of 1.5 m. The narrow overlapping leaves encircle the branches and hang down in graceful festoons with ripe red cones appearing on the curved tips of the branches in season. Its tiny fruit is a black nut sitting in its acorn-like red container. Charcoal made from rimu was sometimes mixed with grease by the Maori to rub into tattoo incisions, thus making indelible markings.

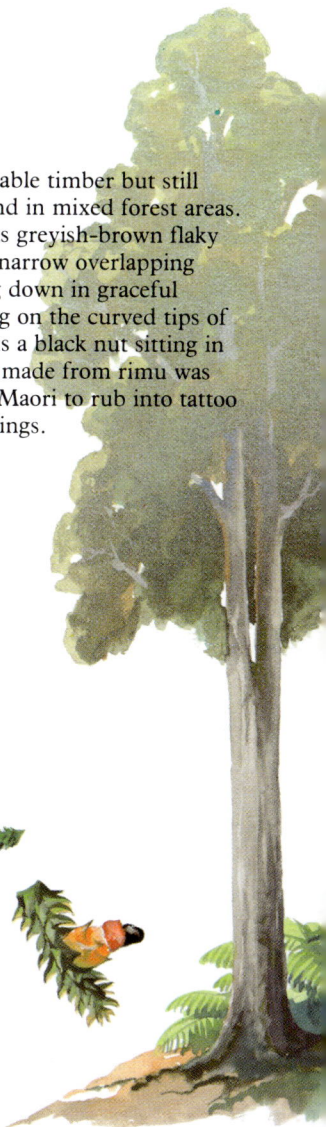

TANEKAHA (Celery pine)

Phyllocladus trichomanoides

Found growing in the northern half of the North Island, Nelson and Northern Marlborough, this tree attains an elevation of 20 m but rarely exceeds 1 m in circumference. Its flat branchlets, which are celery shaped, have the appearance of leaves and act as such; its true leaves are on seedling plants, narrow and round-ended. Small male and female flower cones are on the same tree but separated. The outer grey mottled bark was stripped off by the Maori who used the inner bark to make a red dye. Fish hooks were made from the young twigs and saplings into walking sticks.

TARATA (Lemonwood)

Pittosporum eugenioides

The common name, lemonwood, describes a simple
way to identify the tree: young leaves, bruised between
the fingers, give off a typical lemon fragrance. This tree
has a handsome, widespread shape and it can top 12 m
occasionally. It has a trunk of 60 cm diameter encased
with white bark. The small yellow flowers grow
in large sprays and are of pleasing fragrance.
The Maori used gum from the tarata bark in a
complex scent formula along with parts of other
plants. Like other members of the *pittosporum*
family, the tarata's black seeds are held in their
woody pods by a sticky fluid.

TAUPATA

Coprosma repens

A small shrub or tree standing 8 m tall that is found in coastal regions throughout New Zealand, particularly in the North Island. It is well adapted to stand severe wind and salt spray action. It has a grey coloured trunk branches that twist and turn in irregular form. The leaves are extremely glossy, thick and hairless, with a bright green upper side and a light green reverse. Clusters of glistening orange berries, the size and shape of currants appear between January and April, perhaps compensating for the fact that the green-yellow flowers are inconspicuous and lack a perfume. The berries of the taupata were eaten by the Maori in hard times.

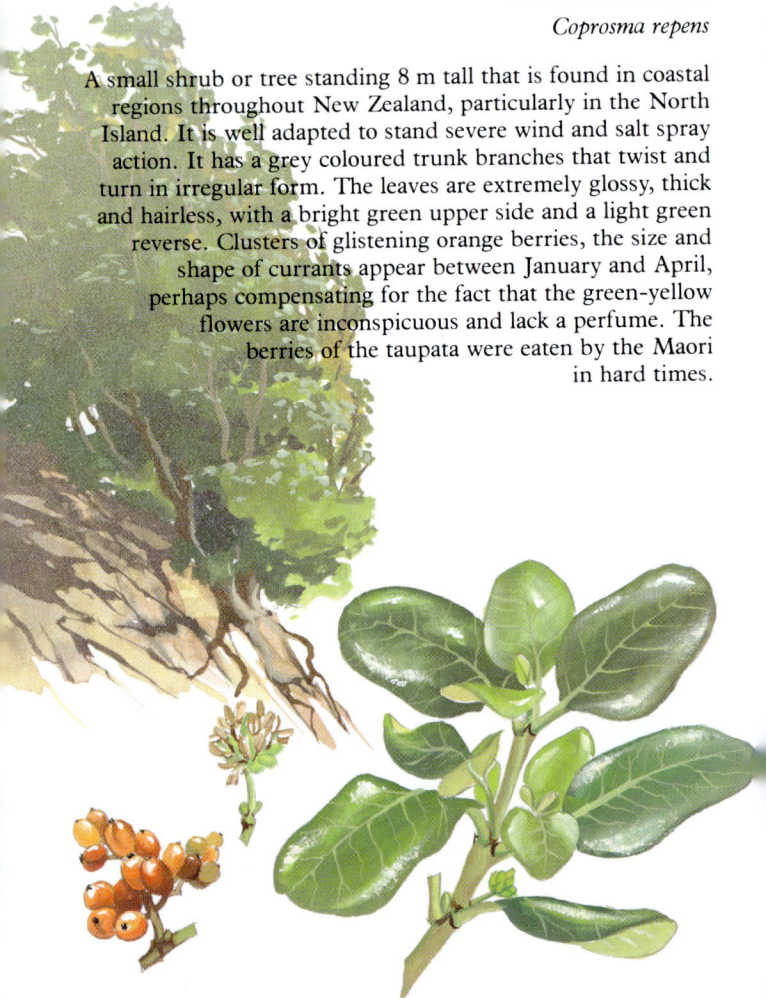

TAWA

Beilschmiedia tawa

Tawa is a common shade-loving lowland tree that prefers rich
soil and is distributed throughout the North Island and in
Nelson and Marlborough. It attains 25 m in height, often
grows in stands of its own species, and has a long straight
and slender trunk of around 1.5 m in diameter with smooth,
thin, blackish bark. The leaves are smooth too, narrow,
lance-shaped and lightly-veined. The flowers are very tiny,
green, and rise in sprays from the axils of the leaves.
Blue-black berries, resembling plums, but more oblong
in shape, were collected by the Maori for food. If picked
fresh they taste strongly of turpentine, but if left for some
time after falling from the tree they become juicy and
refreshing to the palate.

TAWAPOU

Planchonella novo-zelandica

Like the pohutukawa the tawapou tree grows primarily on the sea coast but is limited in its distribution to various coastal regions of the North Island and adjacent islets. Rare and beautiful to look at, this small tree can reach 12 to 15 m and have a trunk 1 m across. Its wood is white in colour, hard and lasting, its leaves leathery and shiny with light undersides. It has small dainty flowers that grow out from the leaf axils in ones and twos. The Maori ate the pulpy flesh of the fruit in olden times and the large polished seeds which range all the way in colour from orange to purple-black provided ornamental necklaces for the chiefs and for their ladies.

TAWHAI (Silver beech)

Northofagus menziesii

Distinguished by its light green foliage and widespread low
hanging branches the silver beech is to be found in stands
in mixed forests throughout the North and South
Islands from sea level and up to the sub-alpine areas, but
is absent around Mount Egmont. Its close relations are
the mountain, red, hard and black beeches. This tree
stands 30 m tall at maturity and has a 2 m diameter trunk
with silvery-grey bark which scales off in large flakes. The
leaves are rounded with strongly serrated margins. The
flowers are small, green and brown, the fruit small and
woody. Maori legend says the sap is red from the
blood of Tuna, part-God, part-man who was
slain by Maui.

TAWHAIRAURIKI (Mountain beech)

Northofagus solandri var. cliffortiodes

Mountain beech is found growing from the central North Island plateau to Foveaux Strait in the South Island. It prefers mountain and sub-alpine areas as the name indicates, often forming a substantial portion of sub-alpine forests.

The tree attains a height of about 15 m with a trunk 1 m thick that is cased in dark brown, smooth bark when the tree is old. It has dark green pointed leaves, in contrast to the light green rounded ones of the silver beech, with white or fawn hairs on the reverse sides. The flowers are small and red, the fruit small and woody.

TI KOUKA (Cabbage tree)

Cordyline austalis

A well-known tree common in open country, moist forests
and swamps from sea level to 600 m and like the nikau palm
adding a touch of the tropics to the New Zealand landscape.
It varies in height from 10 to 20 m. When young it has a
single straight grey coloured trunk. Later it adds stems
growing downwards and its trunk becomes sometimes 1.5 m
through, a mass of loose fibres. 'Cabbage tree' refers to its
shoots explorer Captain Cook and his sailors ate as a vegetable
and compared to cabbage in taste, not to the shape of any part
of the tree. These young shoots develop to long narrow leaves
of up to 100 cm long. Hundreds of white flowers group in
clusters giving off a scent that attacts myriads of insects.

TITOKI

Alectron excelsus

The titoki grows in bush near the coast-line from sea level to 700 m as far south as Banks Peninsula in the South Island. It is a very ornamental tree with smooth black bark, broad-spreading low branches that stay leafy and a rounded head reaching up to 10 m high. The paired leaves are olive-green in colour and strongly veined, the flowers minute in size, red with no petals and formed in attractive sprays. The fruit casts off a brown husk to reveal a pulpy substance of raspberry form, but of brilliant scarlet colour, with a shiny black seed resembling a bead, at its tip. These seeds were pounded by the Maori to obtain oil for use in a perfume and as a medicine.

TOTARA

Podocarpus totara

After the kauri, the totara may be the longest living tree of the New Zealand forest, attaining an age of 1000 and more years. It grows throughout the country and because it has soft, light wood and the required length, was the prime choice of the Maori for their war canoes, often 25 m in length. Its thick brown bark peels off in long strips and was used for basket weaving, torches and as kindling wood. Totara leaves are 2.5 cm long, narrow at both ends and are dull brownish-green. Male and female flower cones are on separate trees and the tiny seeds nest on red or pink stalks to attract the birds.

TUTU

Coriaria arborea

Of eight species of *Coriaria* that grow in New Zealand, one is a tree, *Coriaria arborea*, up to 7 m tall and found throughout the country. Like all in the species, its leaves, shoots and seeds are poisonous to man and animals. Only the juice from the berries was used by the Maori to consume, being most carefully separated from stone and stalk, when it was drunk unfermented or boiled with seaweed to form a palatable jelly. Do not pick and eat the berries from the tree. The paired leaves are dark green and shiny, the tiny yellow flowers droop in long racemes, developing in time to berry-like parts of purple-black colour.

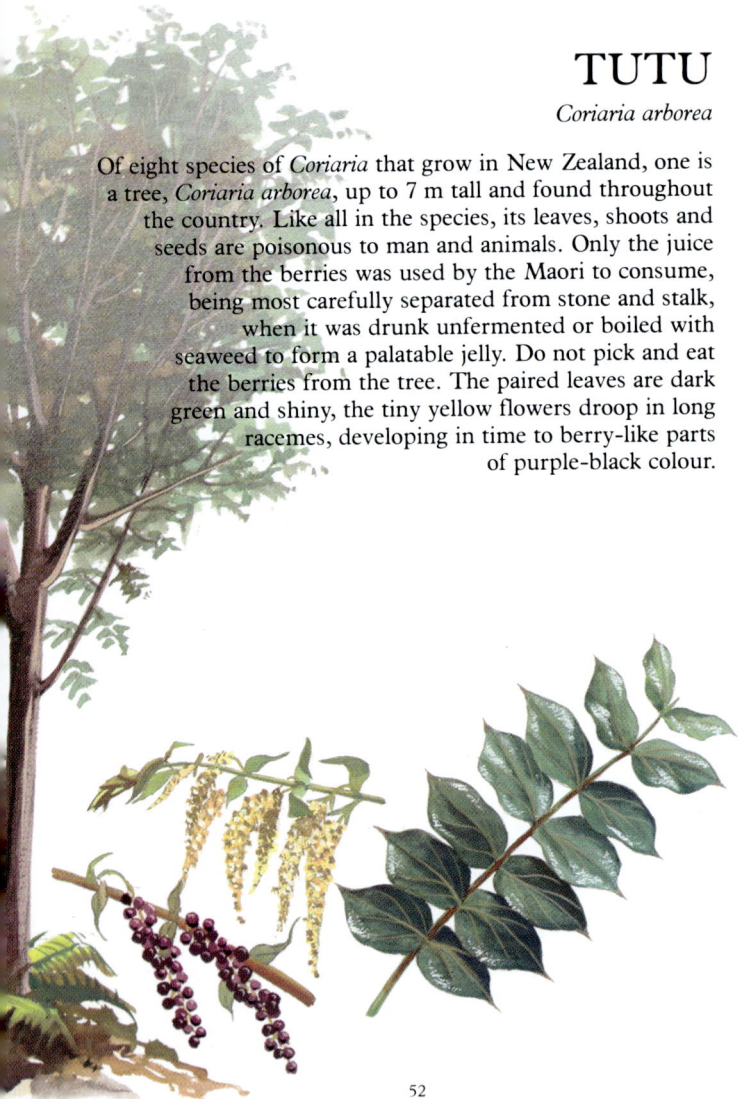

WHARANGI

Melicope ternata

A small tree that is common in the North Island on the coasts and on the edges of lowland forests. It is often many-branched and acquires a rounded top. The leaves are yellowish-green as are the tiny flowers which have the fragrance of violets. The black shiny seeds are contained in brown capsules. From the leaves the Maori made a kind of short dart by taking the wharangi leaf and sticking it into a seed stalk of the karetu grass. According to Maori legend its leaves were used as clothes by spirits.

MAMAKU (Black tree fern)

Sphaeropteris medullaris

Tallest of New Zealand ferns, mamaku grows to 20 m tall
with fronds varying greatly in length, from 2 to 7 m long. It is
found everywhere except Canterbury and Otago. As it
matures this tree fern often acquires aerial root buttresses.
The Maori cooked the upper part of the stem overnight
and ate its soft interior when cold.

KIWIKIWI

Blechnum fluviatile

This hardy fern has short fronds of olive green colour
that often lie touching the ground. It is found throughout
New Zealand on hilly country, preferring damp
situations. A few fronds of this fern were used by Maori
priests to attach to a post in order to
ward off evil spirits.

MOKIMOKI

Doodia caudata

Grows in the North Island in many places, also in Nelson. A small and pretty terrestrial fern, the mokimoki was used to pack around the kumara (sweet potato) in Maori storehouses to the accompaniment of due ceremony. It was also a component in a favourite perfume.

MAUKU (Hen and chickens fern)

Asplenium bulbiferum

A fern for damp locations growing in all parts of the country. The fronds are oval in form and bright green in colour. Identification of the species is assisted by the growth of young plants on the upper surface of its fronds. The young shoots are gathered for the pot by trampers in the bush. They taste like fresh asparagus.

PIUPIU (Crown fern)

Blechnum discolor

Widely distributed throughout New Zealand, this fern often makes up a good part of the ground cover. Its fronds are bright green and up to 1.5 m long. The Maori warriors used to break off and turn upwards the fronds of this fern to mark the trail for a war party — the silvery-grey side being very conspicuous against the dark vegetation of the forest.

PARA (Horseshoe fern)

Marattia salicina

Each bulb or root that attachs to the main stem of this fern looks not unlike the shape of a horseshoe, hence the name. The Maori considered this tuberous mass a great delicacy as it was rare even in olden times. Para has very long fronds, some 2 to 4 m in length. It is found in only a few localities in the North Island.